I0439050

Table of Contents

Introduction

Relevance

The U.S. Army has made significant adaptations to its warfighting skills in response to the operating environment in Iraq and Afghanistan. This adaptation is evident in the implementation of the Army's counterinsurgency doctrine that has guided the brigade combat team's training and preparation in both of these wars over the last 10 years. However, the United States Army is beginning to move away from the current fight in Iraq and Afghanistan. This will mean brigade combat teams will now shift their focus from winning the current fight to preparing for the next possible threat. Although the Army must continue to prepare for ongoing operations, brigade combat teams cannot shortchange their soldiers or the nation with respect to preparing and training for potential combat operations. As General Robert Cone, the Commanding General of the United States Training and Doctrine Command recently stated, "The real art is finding the right balance that allows the Army to succeed in the current fight while simultaneously preparing for the future."[1]

In preparing for the future, the question then becomes what threat should the brigade combat team prepare for and what are the skills it must possess to be successful. The U.S. Army has determined that the brigade combat team should prepare for a hybrid threat when preparing for the future. The United States Army's *2011 Posture Statement* and *U.S. Army Doctrinal Publication 3-0: Operations* state that the hybrid threat will be an adversary who combines the agility and flexibility of being a irregular and decentralized enemy with the power and technology of a nation state. The Army has not specifically provided an answer to the second part of the question, what are the core skills the brigade combat team must possess in order to defeat the hybrid threat? In addition, current U.S. Army training doctrine and Combined Arms Training

---

[1] General Robert W. Cone, "Shaping the Army of 2020," *Army Magazine, October, 2011*, 71.

Strategies do not prioritize or outline the required skill sets required by a brigade combat team to defeat a hybrid threat given the 12-24 month train/ready cycle of the Army Force Generating life cycle.[2]

The sections that follow will make the case that the U.S. Army training doctrine and the Combined Arms Training Strategies does not prioritize or outline the required skill sets required to defeat a hybrid threat. In addition, the author suggests that the 1994/1996 Chechnya Wars and 2006 Lebanon War can be used to identify the fundamental training tasks a brigade combat team should focus on during their train/ready cycle in order to defeat a hybrid threat.[3]

This monograph is broadly organized into six sections. The first section will introduce the reader to U.S. Army training doctrine in order to outline the process a brigade combat team would take in developing a training strategy and the considerations associated with the strategy. Section two will consist of the literature review to broaden the reader's understanding of the hybrid threat. The literature review will provide the reader with an understanding of the organizational structure, capabilities, and techniques and procedures used by hybrid enemies. In sections three and four, the author will analyze the 2006 Lebanon War and 1994/1996 Chechnya Wars. The author will analyze these conflicts to identify patterns where the Israel and Russian armies had difficulty in facing a hybrid threat. Additionally these sections will summarize the readiness conditions the Russian/Israeli forces had prior to the start of the conflicts. The last two sections of this monograph will consist of the conclusion and recommendation. The conclusion will outline the recurring lessons learned from the two military cases and the shortfalls between the lessons

---

[2] The Combined Arms Training Strategies provides standard unit training strategies to support Department of the Army (DA) unit operations and to assist unit commanders in developing unit training plans.

[3] The train/ready cycle is third cycle in the Army Force Generation process of building brigade combat team capacity to conduct full spectrum operations.

2

and U.S. Army training doctrine. Lastly, the author will recommend why these lessons learned should be prioritized in order to train a brigade combat team for a hybrid threat.

U.S. Army Training Doctrine

Before properly understanding what to train for, it is necessary to understand the context of how the Army trains. The Army training system focuses the Army's training efforts in three domains which consist of institutional, self-development, and operational training. These three domains are interdependent and mutually support Army training readiness. The institutional domain is where the Army focuses on training Soldiers and leaders on the key knowledge, skills, and attributes required for the Army Profession of Arms. These are typically the training courses found within the Army's Training Doctrine Command. The self-development domain is where Soldiers and leaders are committed to lifelong, planned, goal oriented learning in order to reach personal and professional goals generally fostering broad multi-disciplinary learning that builds capacity for critical thought. The operational domain is where units and leaders achieve the capabilities to fight and win across the full spectrum of operations. The operational domain has three components: home station training, combat training center training, and training while deployed.[4] For the purposes of this monograph, the author will focus only on home station training within the operational domain. Home station is focused on producing units and leaders capable of executing full spectrum operations in a joint, interagency, intergovernmental, and multinational construct.[5] The focus is on Home station training because this is where the majority of training days occur and where commanders have the most direct influence on deciding training

---

[4] U.S. Army, *The U.S. Army Training Concept, 2012-2020, 2011* (Fort Monroe: Headquarters, Department of the Army, 2011),12.

[5] The focus in on home station training because this is where the majority of training days occur. Combat Training Center rotations are not always part of a train/ready cycle and deployment training is too late to become proficient at a skill set.

3

strategies. Additionally, once deployed–it becomes too little too late to make up for training short falls.

Field Manual 7-0, Training Units and Developing Leaders for Full Spectrum Operations is the Army's keystone doctrine for training units and developing leaders. The purpose of the field manual is to provide the fundamentals of training Army forces and developing leaders to conduct full spectrum operations.[6] The manual does not direct specific tasks for units to train in order build the capability to fight and win across the full spectrum of operations. *Field Manual 7-0* establishes the influences that drive training requirements and capabilities necessary to build and sustain a brigade combat team capable of executing full spectrum operations. *Field Manual 7-0* outlines two variables that help commanders to shape unit training, the characteristics of the operational environment and characteristics of the threat.

Field Manual 7-0 describes the operating environment as chaotic, complex, and uncertain.[7] The Army Capstone Concept expands this further by providing the trends that will generate the uncertain and complex environment. These trends include changing demographics, globalization, economic patterns, emerging technologies, scarcity of food and water, natural disasters, and competition and conflict in the domains of cyber and space (Global Commons). This uncertainty and complexity of the future operational environment will require Army units to respond to a broad range of threats and challenges.[8] The skills required to operate within this type of environment are not addressed.

Field Manual 7-0 goes on to describe the characteristics of the future threat as a hybrid threat. The hybrid threat is a diverse and dynamic combination of regular forces, irregular forces,

---

[6] U.S. Army, *Field Manual 7-0, Training Units and Developing Leaders for Full Spectrum Operations, 2011* (Washington: Headquarters, Department of the Army, 2011), iii.

[7] Ibid, 3-5.

[8] U.S. Army, *The U.S. Army Capstone Concept* (Fort Monroe: Headquarters, Department of the Army, 2011), 9.

4

criminal elements, or any combination of these forces all purposely or loosely unified to achieve a mutually benefitting effect. The manual also states that the brigade combat team could fight several enemies with different goals and capabilities, rather than a single enemy unified by a purpose or command. The brigade combat team's training must account for these influences in order to remain ready to conduct full spectrum operations.[9] Again, the manual does not outline specific skills required to face a hybrid threat. The manual only states that training must account for this type of threat.

The manual also outlines the principles that govern the conduct of military training. The endstate for training is for it to be tough, realistic, standard based, performance oriented training in order to be prepared to conduct full spectrum operations. Brigade combat teams train as they fight. This means training for the mission under the conditions of expected, anticipated, or plausible operational environments.[10] Brigade combat teams train the fundamentals first. *Field Manual 7-0* defines the fundamentals as the warrior tasks and battle drills and the brigade combat teams mission essential task list. All training is organized around the brigade combat team's Full Spectrum Operations Mission Essential Task List. The mission essential tasks are a collection of tasks a unit must be able to perform successfully to accomplish its mission.[11]

In order for the brigade combat team to develop its Full Spectrum Mission Essential Task List, it must take into consideration the operational environment and the threat. These variables assist the brigade combat team commander and subordinate commanders to select the tasks to train. As mentioned earlier, the training manual does not provide the skill sets required for these variables but only a description of them. It does not provide the commander with an assessment or historical example of these two variables interacting on the battlefield. Therefore, the

---

[9] U.S. Army, *Field Manual 7-0, Training Units and Developing Leaders for Full Spectrum Operations, 2011* (Washington: Headquarters, Department of the Army, 2011), 1-2.

[10] Ibid., 2-4.

[11] Ibid., 2-7.

commander must make a subjective decision on what tasks the brigade should train using the Combined Arms Training Strategies. These strategies are a menu of tactical tasks that a brigade combat team might have to execute during full spectrum operations. The lists of tasks are generated by the Combined Arms Center's training directorate at Fort Leavenworth, Kansas. These training strategies are organized by type of unit and echelon level found in the Army. Each echelon provides the commander with a selection of tasks between 100-200 tasks organized by the warfighting functions. There is not a direct explanation between the relationship of the operational environment and the threats described in Field Manual 7-0 and the tactical tasks found in the Combined Arms Training Strategies. The analysis that determines what tasks to train for is based on the brigade combat team's mission. Commanders will vary their selection of tasks based on their personal analysis.[12] *Field Manual 7-0* and the Combined Arms Training Strategies does help the commander with providing academic and professional discourse or a historical military example in order to utilize critical thinking in developing a training strategy for the hybrid threat. The number of collective tasks the brigade combat team is asked to do is overwhelming because of the limited amount of time units have during the train/ready cycle. Operational pace affects every facet of Army life, to include training. The Army Training and Leader Development Panel found that most Army officers believe the Army is trying to do too much with available time to train units. Excessive operational pace is a major source of degradation to the quality of training and leader development. This panel went on to suggest that the Army develop and establish a set of standards that serves as the baseline requirement for operations.[13] These same finding were echoed by the Vice Chief of Staff of the Army, General Lloyd Austin and the Combined Arms Center commander, Lieutenant General David Perkins

---

[12] U.S. Army, *Field Manual 7-0, Training Units and Developing Leaders for Full Spectrum Operations, 2011* (Washington: Headquarters, Department of the Army, 2011), 1-2.

[13] *The Army Training and Leader Development Panel Officer Study, 2009*, (Washington: Headquarters, Department of the Army, 2009), 6.

during a Pre-Command Course to future brigade and battalion commanders.[14] Identifying a baseline of required skill sets in a time constraint environment in order to defeat a hybrid threat is what company commanders are requesting from their senior leadership. This monograph is trying to capture the baseline tasks required to defeat a hybrid threat.

The Army Force Generation Cycle is the last element that affects Army unit training strategy. The Army Force Generation process builds brigade combat team capacity to conduct full spectrum operations. The process consists of three major cycles: (1) reset, (2) train/ready, and (3) available. These cycles have different training and leader development requirements. The reset cycle allows the brigade combat team to refit equipment, conduct new equipment fielding, and receive new Soldiers. There is no collective training above the team and section level within the brigade combat team. The train/ready cycle allows the brigade combat team to achieve proficiency in the collective tasks that support their Full Spectrum Operations Mission Essential Task List. This collective training is focused on a known operational environment or known threat. The key to this cycle is selecting a few tasks to train and replicate. The last cycle of the Army Force Generation Force is available. Brigade combat teams will deploy or continue to build capability to face a hybrid threat.[15] The author is only concerned with the train/ready phase of the Army Force Generation Force for this monograph. The train/ready cycle introduces the training dilemma for commanders. The brigade combat team is limited to the amount of time it can train before it is required to execute a mission or before the life cycle manning begins to transition personnel out while brining in new personnel who were not part of the train up.

Field Manual 7-0 provides just enough guidance to facilitate unit training and leader development. Army training doctrine provides an understanding of how to conduct tough realistic

---

[14] General Austin and Lieutenant General Perkins were guest speakers at the 12-04 Pre-Command Course on March 2, 2012. Both generals briefed results of a recent Inspector General's assessment of company commanders across the Army.

[15] *The Army Training and Leader Development Panel Officer Study,* 3-3-34.

training but falls short of explaining what skills it should develop to defeat a hybrid threat. Doctrine does not provide the brigade commander a tool to narrow down the over 300 collective tasks that can be chosen from the Combined Arms Training Strategies. A baseline of collective skill sets to build upon does not exist. Current doctrine also does not prioritize the required tasks given a train/ready cycle of 12-24 months that brigade combat teams are required to operate within. It is not uncommon to find commanders struggling to define what should the unit train during a training cycle. Training leads to brigade combat teams ability to face their adversaries on the battlefield. The above section provided the understanding of how the brigade combat team prepares itself to be ready to fight and win the United States battles. The next section will inform the reader on who the United States anticipates to be its next adversary.

Hybrid Threat

This monograph will determine the brigade combat team's fundamental training tasks given their 12-24 month training cycle in preparation for the hybrid threat. A key component to answering this research question is defining the hybrid threat. This first section will define and explains the ideas of the hybrid threat. The second section will describe how the threat organizes and how it will conduct warfare.

The term hybrid threat has risen in use in the last several years. It appears in official government reports, articles, and speeches. The 2006 war in Lebanon between Hezbollah and Israel has generated the interest in the concept of a hybrid threat. Literature on the hybrid threat has proliferated since the end of that conflict. The research utilized for this monograph did not find arguments against the concept of a hybrid threat. This does not suggest that an argument against the hybrid threat does not exist. In addition, the purpose of this research is not to debate whether or not the U.S. Army is correct in labeling the future threat as hybrid. However, this literature review is to provide some clarity to the term hybrid threat since there are numerous descriptions that exist in defining what a hybrid threat entails.

Leading the discourse on hybrid threats is Frank Hoffman with his monograph *Conflict in the 21ˢᵗ Century: Rise of the Hybrid Wars*. He believes since the collapse of the Soviet Union, warfare in our time is ever changing. He puts forward the idea that future threats will incorporate a range of different modes of warfare including conventional capabilities, irregular tactics and formations, terrorist acts including indiscriminate violence and coercion, and criminal disorder. Frank Hoffman states that it is too simplistic to merely classify conflict as "Big and Conventional" versus "Small or Irregular." Warfare will be increasingly impossible to characterize states as essentially traditional forces, or non-state actors as inherently irregular. The future will entail conflicts waged by states or political groups, and incorporate a range of different modes of warfare including conventional capabilities, irregular tactics and formations, terrorist acts, and criminal disorder. The future cannot be captured with a simple binary choice of big and conventional versus small and irregular. According to Mr. Hoffmann, the hybrid actors will exploit the modern technologies and present the Western world with asymmetric modes of operations and unanticipated tactics. These actors will not remain static but will continuously evolve and exploit the tactics, techniques, and procedures that offer the greatest return on investment.[16]

The concept of hybrid threats can be found outside the United States defense academia as written in the Australian Army's concept paper *Complex Warfighting*. David Kilcullen states that today's armed forces must deal with adversaries beyond their traditional forms of national armies. These include insurgents, terrorist, criminals, and many other elements.[17] The Australian military has identified a shift in future threat activities. Michael Krause details that in the future, the

---

[16] Frank G. Hoffman, "Conflict in the 21ˢᵗ Century: The Rise of Hybrid Wars," Potomac Institute for Policy Studies, Monograph, (Arlington, 2007), 57-59.

[17] David C. Kicullen, "Complex Warfighting" Future Land Warfare Branch, Royal Australian Army Journal, *www.quantico.usmc.mil/download.aspx?Path=./Uploads/files/SVG_ complex_warfighting.pdf* (accessed January 23, 2012).

blurring of irregular, conventional and high-tech warfare into a hybrid form of complex irregular

warfare will provide a reasonable chance of success for the adversary using all available means.[18]

The hybrid threat can also be found in British defense literature. The United Kingdom's Ministry

of Defense Future "Character of Conflict" paper discusses the increasingly hybrid nature of war.

The paper explains the adversaries of the United Kingdom will exploit their weakness using a

wide variety of high-end and low-end asymmetric techniques. The future conflict will present the

British with adversaries combining conventional, irregular, and high-end asymmetrical threats in

the same time and space.[19]

Subsequent supporting research into the hybrid threat includes key scholars retired U.S.

Army Colonel John McCuen, and Historian Thomas Huber, have endorsed this concept of

blurring future warfare threat categories as highly predictable.[20] Huber explains the phenomena of

regular conventional forces and irregular forces operating under unified direction to accomplish

an endstate provides a mutual accommodation that an adversary employing solely a conventional

force can hardly hope to match.[21] McCuen's defines the threat as an adversary combining both

symmetric and asymmetric war. The conflict of the hybrid threat will be fought not only on the

traditional battlefields, but on asymmetric battleground within the population.[22]

The development of the hybrid threat construct began with the United States 2005

National Defense Strategy. The United States predominance in traditional warfare would force

the enemy to shift from opposing U.S. Forces and to prepare more nontraditional or asymmetric

---

[18] Michael,Krause, "Square Pegs for Round Holes: Current Approaches to future warfare & the Need to Adapt," Land Warfare Studies Centre Working Paper No. 132, (Commonwealth of Australia, June 2007), 19-21.

[19] United Kingdom, Ministry of Defense, "Future Character of Conflict," HQ Land Forces, 2010, http://www.mod.uk/DefenseInternet/MicroSite/DCDC/\(accessed January 23, 2012).

[20] David E. Johnson, *Military Capabilities for a Hybrid War*, (Santa Monica: RAND, 2010), 5-10.

[21] Thomas M. Huber, *Compound Warfare: That Fatal Knot* (Fort Leavenworth, KS: US Army Command and Staff College Press, 2002), vii.

[22] John C. McCuen, Colonel (R) "Hybrid Wars," *Military Review* (April-May 2008), 108.

methods. The National Defense Strategy framed the future threat into four challenges with distinct capabilities and methods. These challenges included traditional challenges posed by states employing recognized military capabilities in well-understood forms of military conflict. Irregular challenges would come from those employing unconventional methods to counter traditional advantages of stronger opponents. Catastrophic challenges involved those acquiring, possessing, and using weapons of mass destruction. Lastly, disruptive challenges would include those enemies who would use technology to negate current United States advantages.[23]

Currently the Army defines the hybrid threat as a diverse and dynamic combination of regular forces, irregular forces, and/or criminal elements all unified to achieve mutually benefitting effects. The characteristics of the threat include innovation, adaptability, and networking at both global and local levels. These threats possess a wide range of old and new technologies. The tactics include operating conventionally and unconventionally by employing adaptive and asymmetric combinations of traditional, irregular, and criminal tactics. The hybrid threat's purpose is to create multiple dilemmas for its opponent.[24] The dilemma is created by establishing a network of people, capabilities, and devices that merge, split, and coalesce in actions across all of the operational variables of the operational environment. The threat is attempting to create severe impacts across the entire operational environment to prevent its threat from segregating the conflict into easily assailable parts.[25] This monograph will define the hybrid threat as any adversary that simultaneously and adaptively employs a fused mix of conventional weapons, irregular tactics, terrorism, and criminal behavior in the battle space to obtain their political objectives.

---

[23] U.S. Department of Defense, *National Defense Strategy,* 2005, (Washington: Department of Defense, 2005), 2.

[24] U.S. Army, *Training Circular 7-100, Hybrid Threat, 2010* (Washington: Headquarters, Department of the Army, 2011), 1-1.

[25] Ibid., 1-2.

Hybrid Threat Organization and Tactics

All the above mentioned authors or literature communicate that the hybrid threat will or can consists of many different actors. These actors include military forces, nation state paramilitary forces, insurgent groups, guerilla units, and criminal organizations. Hoffman states that the intervening force could expect to see conventional and irregular tactic, techniques and procedures, all manner of terrorist acts targeting not only military but also civilian populace, an increase use of crime as a weapon system, an emphasis placed on cyber war, and an exploitation of the media.[26] Regular military forces are the regulated armed forces of a state with the specialized function of military offensive and defensive capabilities with legitimate service to the state or alliance. Insurgents are groups or movements that seek to overthrow or force change of a governing authority. Insurgent organizations do not have a regular table of organization and equipment structure. A guerilla is a combat participant in military operations conducted in enemy held or hostile territory by irregular indigenous forces. Criminal organizations are normally independent of nation state control.[27]

The hybrid actor will attempt to destroy or neutralize vulnerable single points of failure in the opponent's warfighting functions.[28] It will accomplish this by using systems warfare. A system is a set of different elements so connected or related as to perform a unique function not performable by the elements or components alone. The hybrid actor views the operational environmental system composed of subsystems and components. The primary principle of

---

[26] Frank G. Hoffman, "Conflict in the 21st Century: The Rise of Hybrid Wars," Potomac Institute for Policy Studies, Monograph, (Arlington, 2007), 17-35.

[27] Russel W. Glenn, "Thoughts on Hybrid Conflict," *Small Wars Journal* http://www.smallwarsjournal.com (accessed December 18, 2011).

[28] Frank G. Hoffman, "Hybrid Threats: Reconceptualizing the Evolving Character of Conflict," *Strategic Forum*, (April 2005), 5.

systems warfare is the identification and isolation of the critical subsystems or components that give the opponent the capability and cohesion to achieve the threat's objectives.[29]

The opponent's most challenging aspect when facing a hybrid threat will be the threat's ability to adapt and transition. The threat defeats a larger and powerful opponent by using speed, agility, and versatility. Opponents of the hybrid threat will have difficulty isolating specific challenges. An opponent will be forced to conduct economy of force measures on one or more lines of operations. The hybrid actors will meanwhile continue to shift the effort and emphasis to make the decision process difficult for the opponent. [30] Hybrid actors do not require quick success. It attempts to wear down the popular support for the opponent while not attempting to lose the war, hybrid actors seek to operate along multiple lines of operations in an effort to reduce the opponent's ability to concentrate combat power. It attempts to present the opponent with a complex problem by stretching resources, restricting freedom of maneuver, and reducing intellectual capacity. It does this by creating economic instability, fostering lack of trust in existing governance, attacking information networks, causing man made humanitarian crises, and physically endangering opponents. In the end, hybrid actors see conflict holistically and do not break it up into convenient pieces.[31]

The hybrid actors will transition in and out of its various forms. Military forces can remove uniforms and other indicators and blend into the local population. Insurgent forces can abandon weapons and protest innocence of wrongdoing. Criminals can impersonate local police forces in order to gain access to key facilities. The opponent of the hybrid threat will have difficulty indentifying the threat.

---

[29] United Kingdom, Ministry of Defense, "Future Character of Conflict" HQ Land Forces, 2010, http://www.mod.uk/DefenseInternet/MicroSite/DCDC/\(accessed January 23, 2012).

[30] U.S. Army, *Training Circular 7-100, Hybrid Threat, 2011* (Washington: Headquarters, Department of the Army, 2010), 1-3.

[31] Ibid., 1-2.

The 2006 Lebanon War and 1994/1996 Chechnya Wars will be assessed in the next two sections of the monograph to help identify the fundamental skill sets a brigade combat team should train on in order to defeat a hybrid threat. Current scholars on the subject of hybrid threats use the 1994/1996 Chechnya War and 2006 Lebanon War as recent examples of hybrid warfare. These conflicts provide examples of the hybrid threat's tactics, techniques, and procedures used on the battlefield. Additionally, these conflicts show the difficulties that the Russians and Israelis encountered while fighting this type of threat. The aim of these sections is to provide perspective on insights from these two hybrid wars. These sections will provide the reader with an overview of the conflict; identify the difficulties that both Israel and Russia had in facing a hybrid threat, and their implication for the brigade combat team concerning training.

2006 Lebanon War

Overview

The Lebanon war of 2006 was a 34-day conflict in Lebanon, Northern Israel, and Israeli occupied territories. The conflict started on 12 July 2006, when Hezbollah fired Katyusha rockets and mortars at an Israeli position, diverting attention, in order to allow them to cross the border to abduct Israeli soldiers. The result was two Israeli soldiers were abducted and three others killed. The purpose of the attack was retaliation against Israel holding Samir Kuntar (Palestinian Liberation Front member) as a detainee. Hezbollah's leader, Hassan Nassrallah had pledged earlier to attack Israel if Kuntar was not released. Israel reacted to the attack by launching a large-scale air attack targeting Hezbollah's long-range rocket launchers, observation posts along the border, and compounds believed to be used to cross into Israel. Hezbollah in return, fired rockets towards Israel. Hezbollah would continue to fire 100 or more rocket attacks a day for 22 of the 34 days of the conflict.[32]

Israel continued its attack on Hezbollah by conducting a ground attack into the village of Marun ar Ras in Lebanon on June 28, 2006. This village was chosen because it sat on high ground that controlled much of the border. By the end of July, the Israel Defense Force would conduct several other operations around Lebanese towns of Bint Jbeil, Marwahin, Kafr Kila, and Tayyibah, which were also along the border. On July 31, Israel launched a new operation designed to create a security zone along the border. By August 9, the Israel Defense Forces were operating in almost every town along the border as far North as Qantarah and as far South as Dibil. On August 11, Israel would launch their final ground assault. Israeli forces would advance an armored brigade from Tayyibeh westward along the Litani River to the towns of Frun and Ghanduriyih. This unit would link up with troops who were airlifted into these towns. Hezbollah reacted by regrouping in Ghanduriyih and the surrounding area throughout the final days of the conflict.[33] Fighting between Israel and Hezbollah would continue in and around these towns until the end of the conflict. The conflict ended when the United Nations brokered a ceasefire for the morning of 14 August 2006, though it formally ended three weeks later on 8 September when Israel lifted its naval blockade of Lebanon.[34] In 34 days of fighting, the Israel Defense Force lost 119 soldiers while Hezbollah lost an estimated 650-750 fighter.[35]

---

[32] Gilbert Achcar and Michel Warschawski, *The 33-Day War: Israel's War on Hezbollah in Lebanon and Its Consequences* (Boulder: Paradigm Publishers, 2007), 1–36.

[33] Stephen Biddle and Jeffrey A. Friedman, *The 2006 Lebanon Campaign and the Future of Warfare: Implications for Army and Defense Policy* (Carlisle, PA: US Army War College, Strategic Studies Institute, 2008) 29-33.

[34] Achcar and Warschawski, *The 33-Day War*, 31–36.

[35] Ibid.

Israel Defense Force before the 2006 Lebanon War

Israel's security situation before 2006 demanded that it conduct counterinsurgency operations against the Palestinians. The mindset of the military focused on low intensity conflict. At no stage was an Israeli unit required to face an enemy force any larger than an infantry squad.[36] The Army's active and reserve soldiers had not executed any major training exercises focused on conventional war fighting skills for five years before the 2006 war against Hezbollah. Battalion size units and smaller had not conduct combined arms maneuver training prior to the Israel Defense Force employment of ground forces in the 2006 war.[37] This created challenges for junior officers and inhibited their ability to adapt from fighting low intensity conflict warfare to fighting against a hybrid threat.[38]

Hezbollah Assessment

Hezbollah is an adversary more in the middle range that spans the spectrum of conflict from irregular warfare to major combat operations—neither an irregular opponent nor a conventional force. Hezbollah operated in a manner compatible with the battlefield conditions.[39] Hezbollah used a more blended form of operations. Hezbollah did not use classical guerrilla tactics, though one would think that Hezbollah would utilize classical guerrilla techniques when confronted by superior firepower.

Hezbollah fought engagements far longer than one would expect from guerrillas with no intention of holding ground. However, Hezbollah combat engineers constructed defensive positions across the towns of southern Lebanon. Outposts were dispersed, yet integrated company

---

[36] David E. Johnson, *Military Capabilities for a Hybrid War*, (Santa Monica: RAND, 2010), 2-3.

[37] Matt Matthews, *We Were Caught Unprepared: The 2006 Hezbollah-Israeli War* (Fort Leavenworth, KS: U.S. Army Combined Arms Center Combat Studies Institute Press, 2008), 6-9.

[38] Avi Kober, "The Israeli Defense Forces in the Second Lebanon War: Why the Poor Performance," *Journal of Strategic Studies*, 31:1 (June 2008): 13-15.

[39] Ibid.

sized positions, which included primary, secondary, and decoy positions. For example, at Marun ar Ras, Hezbollah defenders fought for more than 6 hours. In Bint Jubayl, Hezbollah defenders fought for more than 4 days with individual engagements exceeding more than 8 hours. This also suggests that Hezbollah engaged in a substantial amount of close combat that is more familiar with defensive operations conducted by a traditional army. Hezbollah defenders frequently held their positions and continued to fire even after Israel Defense Forces closed to very short ranges. Conventional militaries would expect guerilla forces to inflict casualties at minimum cost and risk to them, and then withdraw, rarely allowing a superior force to close with them. Again, at Muran ar Ras, Hezbollah soldiers fought room to room with Israel Defense Forces and held their positions. These extended engagements suggest that Hezbollah was attempting to hold ground like classical offense and defensive operations.[40] Hezbollah was well prepared to fight the Israel Defense Forces.

Additionally, Hezbollah showed it possessed the ability to tactically maneuver under fire and defend a strong point. This was evident in Hezbollah's counter attacks. Hezbollah attempted to retake lost positions. Classical guerrillas seek attrition of the enemy but not the retention of ground. Guerrillas used counterattacks very sparingly. However, Hezbollah conducted engagements to deliberately attempt to close with Israeli forces in positions recently taken by the forces in attempt to regain lost ground. At Bint Jubayl, a detachment of 60 fighters attacked Israeli defenses. The attackers divided into main and secondary group supported by anti-tank guided missiles with some sporadic indirect fire to support the attack. The attack closed within 10 meters of the Israeli positions before being driven back.[41] Though Hezbollah was turned back,

---

[40] Stephen Biddle and Jeffrey A. Friedman, *The 2006 Lebanon Campaign and the Future of Warfare: Implications for Army and Defense Policy* (Carlisle, PA: US Army War College, Strategic Studies Institute 2008) 34-35.

[41] Ibid, 38-30.

they gave Israel a substantial infantry and anti-armor fight that showed their skills in fire and maneuver.[42]

Hezbollah soldiers were able to utilize effective fires during this conflict. Hezbollah maintained a steady stream of Katyusha rockets throughout the conflict. They launched close to 4,000 rockets during the conflict. Hezbollah demonstrated the ability to integrate fires into their maneuver operations. They successfully integrated anti-armor fires with machinegun fires, which provided cover for repositioning subsequent anti-armor ambushes. Hezbollah was also able to isolate Israeli infantry and armor formations. In the close fight, Hezbollah employed anti armor guided missiles using a 5-6 man team. The teams would allow the Israel Defense Force tanks to pass by and then engage them from the rear.

Hezbollah also understood the value of operating close to the populace. Hezbollah utilized hiding tactics designed to force Israel to abstain from attacking due to fear of collateral causalities. Hezbollah fighters tried to blend in with the civilians and used residential structures for firing positions and hideouts. For example, Hezbollah placed rocket launchers in firing positions next to residential buildings or hid them inside garages between firing missions.[43]

Hezbollah also controlled the information environment. Hezbollah focused on highlighting their battlefield successes and Lebanese civilian causalities and infrastructure damage. Hezbollah accomplished this by utilizing its own television, radio, and internet sites and collaborating with other like-minded Islamist groups. Their greatest victory in the information environment was the destruction of the myth of Israel's battlefield invincibility. Hezbollah was

---

[42] Lieutenant Colonel Scott C. Farquhar, *Back to Basics: A Study of the Second Lebanon War and Operation CASTLEAD* (Fort Leavenworth,KS: U.S. Army Combined Arms Center Combat Studies Institute Press, 2009), 64.

[43] Ibid, 62.

able to survive against Israel while gaining international and regional recognition of its military skills.[44]

Lastly, Hezbollah utilized primitive means. Hezbollah utilized Improvised Explosive Devices and land mines across Southern Lebanon. These mines were emplaced along main roads coupled with rocket attacks limited the Israeli forces the ability to maneuver and destroyed many of their tanks.

Israel Defense Force Assessment

Failure to prepare undercut Israeli operations from the start. Before the war, Israeli planners had unrealistic expectations about armed conflict with Hezbollah. They planned for small skirmishes, not for a large-scale, conventional military campaign. Israeli troops became used to confronting a numerically inferior and poorly trained and equipped enemy. Additionally, Israeli forces became accustomed to having excellent tactical and operational intelligence, massive logistical, technical support, and a familiarity with the combat environment in which they were fighting for many years.[45] The Army fell into a syndrome of planning and preparing to fight the last war.

Over-reliance on airpower provided a false sense of security. While the Israel Defense Forces had long invested in its airpower, until the 1990s, it believed land forces to be critical for victory. Among political leaders, airpower is especially tempting. It offers great destructive capability without a high risk of friendly casualties. Maj. Gen. (res.) Eitan Ben-Eliyahu, former chief of the Israeli air force, admitted that the fixation with new technologies was addictive and

---

[44] Ibid., 66.

[45] Avi Kober, "The Israeli Defense Forces in the Second Lebanon War: Why the poor performance," *Journal of Strategic Studies*, 31:1 (June 2008): 13-15.

obscured Israel's thinking.[46] The land forces lack the training experience of combined arms maneuver. Units lack the ability to integrate field artillery and air assets into the maneuver forces. The field artillery and air targets were focused on preplanned targets and not targets of opportunity developed during the conduct of operations.

Lessons Learned

This 2006 campaign is an example of a non-state actor waging a state like conventional war. Hezbollah did not conform to the ideal model of irregular warfare. It was not a classical guerrilla army, it placed too much emphasis on holding ground, and its forces were concentrated. However, Hezbollah did not exhibit pure conventional methods. It still relied on harassing fires, coercion, and it lacked a sizeable reserve.

Hezbollah engaged Israeli forces in major combat operations as seen in the above battles of Muran ar Ras and Bint Jubayl. Hezbollah's military behavior in these battles exhibited many characteristics that would be expected of a conventional military power. These characteristics include use of cover and concealment, preparation of fighting positions, direct fire discipline, and coordination of indirect fire support. This allowed Hezbollah to inflict more Israeli casualties per Arab fighter in 2006 than did any Israeli opponent did in 1956, 1967, 1973, or 1982 Arab-Israeli conflicts. Their skills in the conventional war fighting were imperfect–but they were also well within the observed bounds of Israeli historical opponents.

To cope with an opponent like Hezbollah who blends guerilla and conventional methods requires forces that can close with and defeat opponents. The basics of combined arms maneuver are necessary for successful operations against threats with capabilities like Hezbollah. These capabilities include a mix of standoff fires and traditional infantry, armor, and artillery–that

---

[46] Eitan Ben-Eliyahu, public lecture, Tel Aviv University, Dec. 19, 2006; Meir Finkel, "The Rites of Technology in the IDF—Return the Balance to the Land Build-Up," *Maarachot*,(June 2006): pp. 40-5.

enable it to combine fire and movement and overcome opponents who mastered enough of the modern systems available to them. Hezbollah created a challenge that demanded combined arms fire and maneuver. The Israeli's lost this skill set after years of preparing for and confronting terrorist attacks prior to the 2006 conflict.[47] The United States Army might be approaching a condition similar to that of the Israelis with the focus on preparing Soldiers for duty in Iraq and Afghanistan over the last ten years. More specifically, the needs for successful operations where heavy forces use infantry complementing tanks in urban and other complex terrain.

The 2006 Lebanon war shows the need to maintain an emphasis on urban operations. The urban terrain provided the backdrop for the conflict. Both Hezbollah and Israeli forces actions were conducted among the people. The last battle within the war was fought in the villages of Jbeil, Marwahin, Kafr Kila, and Tayyibah because they were key terrain along the border. This is an important factor to acknowledge. Current world demographic trends suggest that increasingly the population of the world will be urban. Thus, the likelihood of any military operation being conducted in urban areas is also increasing. Urban fighting has been, and will continue to be a great equalizer. Urban operations will likely be one of the asymmetric strategies of choice for a future adversary who faces an opponent who is has a stronger conventional force. The need for the U.S. Army to conduct stability operations will also take place in urban areas.

In addition, Hezbollah engaged the Israeli forces in small dispersed and shielded units utilizing hit and run tactics that denied easy targets which limited Israel's intelligence, surveillance, and reconnaissance effectiveness. Hezbollah understood the value of "hugging" or hiding tactics designed to force Israel from attacking due to fear of collateral casualties. Hezbollah dispersed their rocket launchers into the urban setting to maximize shielding. Hezbollah fighters blended in with the population effectively. Some did use civilian clothing for deception. Hezbollah also wore uniforms similar to the Israelis in order to make themselves look

---

[47] David E. Johnson, *Military Capabilities for a Hybrid War*, (Santa Monica: RAND, 2010), 7.

like Israeli forces from a distance to cause the Israelis to hesitate before firing. Hezbollah exploited any built up area and familiar terrain as fortresses or ambush sites to mitigate Israeli armor, air mobility, superior firepower, and sensors. The ability to conduct reconnaissance to develop the situation against an adaptive enemy like Hezbollah in complex environments will not only include the employment of technology, but also the ability to conduct reconnaissance in close contact with the enemy and civilian populace. An opponent of a hybrid threat must be able to develop the situation and collect intelligence through physical reconnaissance and human intelligence. It must have a force capable of conducting ground reconnaissance. Because of the shielding and propensity to operate among the people, reconnaissance units will have to fight for information and adapt continuously to the changing situations in order to provide the required intelligence to the commander in order to make the optimal decision.

Three months before the outbreak of the Lebanon war, Israel Defense Forces published new operational doctrine. This doctrine was heavily technology-oriented. It stressed the use of firepower over maneuver, focusing on achieving battlefield success via a combination of accurate, stand-off fire and limited operations on the ground. The operation order issued by the General Staff on 13 July 2006 described the upcoming operation as a stand-off, fire based protracted offense. The Israel Defense Forces Chief of Staff, Dan Halutz, believed in obtaining victory via massive firepower. [48] As the war progressed, it became evident there was a great disproportion between the number of air sorties and fire missions and their impact on Israeli intended results. Hezbollah's capability to carry on the fight and keep launching hundreds of Katyusha rockets onto Israeli territories daily disproved victory would be obtained by fire power alone. Israeli forces were not effective in eliminating Hezbollah targets until they could use air

---

[48] Winograd Commission results,
http://www.mfa.gov.il/MFA/MFAArchive/2000_2009/2008/Winograd%20Committee%20submits%20fina l%20report%2030-Jan-2008 (accessed 11 February, 2012).

and field artillery to support the infantry's maneuvers in order to close with and destroy Hezbollah objectives.

Chechnya War

Overview

Tensions between Russia and Chechnya came to a tipping point in December 1994 when Russian soldiers entered Grozny, the capital of Chechen. The Russian soldiers did not expect resistance. They were confident that Chechen rebels would not fight because the rebels were untrained and unorganized. In addition, the presence of Russian tanks would be sufficient in forcing them to back down. It did not take the Russians long to realize their assumption was wrong. The Russian Army would fight block by block for 19 days. The first battle of Grozny concluded on 13 February 1995. The Russians suffered fatalities that included more than 1,000 killed, 84 soldiers captured, and over 200 armored vehicles destroyed. Although the Russians eventually managed at take control of the city, the victory was short- lived. A rebel counter attack would follow which would lead to a negotiated settlement in the fall of 1996.[49]

In December 1999 Russian troops would again entered Grozny. As they had five years before, they proved unprepared for the strength and competence of their enemy. To avoid the dangers of urban combat, the Russians planned to use artillery and air strikes to force their enemy into submission. The Chechens prepared a defense by building underground tunnels and bunker that would mitigate the effects these strikes. The Chechens would hold out until the Russian forces made their way into the city. The war would end again with a truce in August of 1999.[50]

---

[49] Olga Oliker, *Russia's Chechen Wars 1994-2000*, (Santa Monica: RAND, 2001), 1-2.

[50] Ibid.

Russian Army before the Chechnya War

The Russian forces were designed to wage a high intensity and technological war. The Army was intended to deliver an overwhelming armored attack in the initial phases of war, backed by a capability to continue to generate forces over a prolonged period. The experiences of the Afghan War from 1979-1989 did not alter the Russian Army with the preoccupation with large-scale conventional or tactical nuclear warfare. Counterinsurgency, peacekeeping, and other tasks were not featured in Soviet military education.[51]

The Russian Army also suffered a lack of *espirit de corps* and military bearing due to being a conscript army. According to official figures, there were more than 3,000 deaths a year as a result. A high proportion died in accidental deaths due to the failure of the officer corps' to properly supervise their soldiers. Others died because of disease due to sub standard living conditions. Lastly, suicides were a big cause for the deaths. The Russian Army's lack of a professional Non-Commissioned Officer is often cited for poor discipline and low morale which set the conditions for a high suicide rate.[52]

Chechen Rebels Assessment

The Chechen forces were well armed by 1994. The Chechens obtained 40-50 T-62 and T-72 tanks, 20-25 multiple rocket launchers, 30-35 armored personnel carriers, 30 122mm howitzers, and 40-50 BMP infantry fighting vehicles. The Chechens were highly motivated, familiar with the urban terrain, and organized into small, mobile fighting units. Many Chechens had served in the Russian armed forces, hence they were familiar with Russian weapons, spoke the language, and understood the Russian tactics. Most sources state that there were no more than 3,000 Chechen forces in the field at any one time. Russians estimated the number to be 15,000.

---

[51] MJ Orr, *The Russian Ground Forces & Reform 1992-2002*, (Conflict Studies Research Institute Centre, 2003), 6-8.

[52] Ibid.

The Chechens were motivated by a unified common cause and values and embodied a warrior ethos.[53]

The Chechen fighters would respond to immediate threats then put aside their arms to return to their daily business when the fighting stopped. The Chechen's received manpower from outside their borders. The war was considered an Islamic Jihad; therefore, an unknown number of pro–Chechen fighters entered Chechnya to defend against the Russian attack. These fighters have been said to come from Afghanistan, Azerbaijan, Sudan, Ukraine, India, Pakistan, Iraq, and even Russia.

Chechen fighters weakened and delayed the Russian Army lines of communication toward Grozny. They used protesting civilians along the Russian Army's axis of advance toward Grozny causing the Russians to lose their initiative and element of surprise. Additionally, the Chechens used point ambushes on trail elements of march units in order to continue to disrupt the Russian Army's formations and tempo.[54]

The basic unit formation was approximately a squad size element of 8-10 men, typically armed with 1-2 anti tank weapons, a light machine gun, and 1-2 sniper rifles. The remainder carried AK-47s. The Chechen regulars were organized into a platoon sized unit of 20-30 men. They were further organized into company-sized units. Unlike the Russian companies, these units could and did operate independently. These organizations allowed the Chechens to conduct a mobile defense in depth. This tactic was to counter the overwhelming numbers of the Russian Army.[55]

---

[53] Anatol Lieven, *Chechnya: Tombstone of Russian Power*, (New Haven: Yale University Press,1998), 109.

[54] Ib, Faurby, "The Battle(s) of Grozny," *Baltic Defense Review*, (1999): 79-82.

[55] Knezys and Sedlickas, *The War in Chechnya*, (College Station, Texas A&M: University Press, 2000), 95.

Russian Army Assessment

The Russian Army's readiness could be described as poor. The soldiers had little education and lacked moral character. Suicide was rampant and there was a wide-spread desire not to fight within the ranks. Almost one third of conscripts had prior criminal records. The overall army had insufficient logistical support and was poorly trained.

The Russian Army had not conducted a single divisional training exercise between 1992-1994. Russian officers admitted that there were soldiers who had never fired their weapons and others who had not fired on a range since 1992. Russian soldiers were also untrained on more advance equipment like night vision equipment, armored vehicles, and other advanced weaponry. Additionally, the Russian Army was not ready for urban operations. Most officers and nearly all the soldiers had no training in urban operations. The Russian Army did not conduct urban training in the field because of lack of funding. This was considered specialized training, and was one of the first things to be canceled when funds ran low.[56]

The Russian Air Force established air supremacy within two days by destroying Chechnya's few aircraft, airfields, tank motor pools, and major roads. The air campaign however did not meet its objectives. The attacks reinforced the Chechen fighter morale to fight and destroyed any lingering Russian support that might have existed in Chechnya. Russian air attacks destroyed many civilian targets because of poor target discrimination. The Chechen fighters just moved to the Caucasus Mountains for cover. Prior to the Chechnya War, the Russian Army had little experience with handling independent media and was not concerned with public opinion. They made few attempts to control or influence media on the battlefield. The Chechen fighters willingly took the media in and spread the Chechen side of the story for the world to see.[57]

---

[56] Olga Oliker, *Russia's Chechen Wars 1994-2000*, (Santa Monica: RAND, 2001), x.

[57] Ibid, 10.

Ground reconnaissance elements were hard pressed to provide assault units with accurate information. Ground reconnaissance efforts in Grozny often occurred too late and with insufficient focus. Inadequate maps and reporting hampered intelligence gathering. The Russian reconnaissance units lacked aggressiveness. Instead of dismounting and searching for the enemy, the scouts would not go outside of their armored vehicles because of the threat of snipers. In essence, the reconnaissance units only reported what they saw; these units did not attempt to gather and report sufficient information to ensure the Russian Army was not caught by surprise by the Chechen fighters. The Russian Army lacked the understanding the actual intentions and capabilities of the Chechen fighters because of the lack of reconnaissance effort.[58]

The Russians failed to properly plan and rehearse before entering Grozny in 1994. The order to assault Grozny came from Boris Yeltsin on 25 December 1994. On 28 December 1994, Russian forces commenced their attack. Two days was an insufficient amount of time to allow dissemination of a plan from operational level staff, let alone enough time to complete subordinate plans and rehearsals.[59]

Lessons Learned

Small unit formations facilitate ease of movement and maneuver. Small groups allowed the Chechen fighter to blend in with the local populace. This made target discrimination difficult for Russian soldiers. Small mobile formations allowed the Chechens to establish strong point defenses in depth while still giving them the ability to displace and reinforce other defenses. This caused the Russians to overestimate the Chechen size and made it difficult to determine their exact locations. The small groups also gave the Chechens the ability to hug the Russian forces;

---

[58] Knezys and Sedlickas, *The War in Chechnya,* (College Station, Texas A&M: University Press, 2000), 80.

[59] Ibid., 91.

this mitigated the usefulness of Russians indirect fires.[60] The actions taken by the Chechens will require units in contact to assume risk and spread out across the battlefield. The hybrid actor, like the Chechen fighter, will avoid their opponent's strength and look to "bleed their opponent by a thousand cuts." The future battlefield will require brigade combat teams to assume risk and spread out across the battlefield, which in some cases prevents quick reaction, mutually supporting efforts, and clear knowledge of where all forces are at in time of crisis. Brigade combat teams cannot become over dependent on technology or incapable of acting independently. Mission command must be emphasized and taught in order to allow the lower levels of the brigade combat team to take the initiative and responsibility to face a decentralized enemy. This means that brigade combat team leadership must recognize the requirement for decentralized authority that enables subordinates to develop the situation through action, consistent with intent of their leadership.[61]

The most successful technique used by the Chechens involved destroying the lead and trail vehicles in a convoy to prevent the Russians from escaping the kill zone. The Chechens also knew that when the Russian soldiers dismounted, it was better to shoot to wound than to kill. This created more confusion than killing the soldiers. The Russian Army adapted to this technique. They learned to lead with infantry in front of the infantry fighting vehicles and tanks. The infantry would clear and secure buildings to protect the vehicles from top and flank shots where they were vulnerable to anti-tank fires.[62] Combined arms maneuver that integrated fire and maneuver, employing appropriate combination of infantry, mobile protected firepower, offensive and defensive fires, engineers, aviation, and joint capabilities ensure success against techniques utilized by the Chechens.

---

[60] Olga Oliker, *Russia's Chechen Wars 1994-2000*, (Santa Monica: RAND, 2001), 22.

[61] Major General Robert B. Brown, 9 as 1: Small Unit Leadership Development- A Paradigm Shift, *The Cavalry & Armor Journal*, (November-December, 2011) 30.

[62] Oliker, *Russia's Chechen Wars*, 14-22

The shortfalls in the Russian's maneuver and protection warfighting function could have been averted through improved intelligence. The first step in any battle should be to gather all necessary information on the enemy and terrain in which soldiers will fight. The brigade combat team requires the capability to access data and information in an integrated form from numerous collection assets to develop the intelligence and degree of understanding necessary for successful operations against a hybrid threat. Tactical intelligence did not gather this information in detail for the Russians. The Russians did not have the detailed information required to fight in Grozny. Because of poor intelligence and reconnaissance failures, Russian military planners had not realized that the Chechens had been preparing for months to defend Grozny, that indeed they had tanks, rocket launchers, and anti-aircraft units and were ready to put up a fight. Additionally, the Russians lacked demographic intelligence. The army was unprepared for the presence of civilians on the battlefield.[63] The degree of understanding against an adaptive enemy organization like the Chechen Rebels requires not only the employment of technology, but also the conduct of reconnaissance and the development of intelligence in close contact with the enemy and civilian populations. The future combat team must be able to develop the situation and collect intelligence through physical reconnaissance and human intelligence.

Lastly, according to numerous professional observers, Russian's failures were a result of poor coordination of forces. Russian troops lacked a clear chain of command; therefore, resulting in dissention among the various levels and branches of command. Different high-ranking commanders often gave contradictory orders to the same subordinates. The identity of those holding the highest levels of command in Chechnya would change frequently. In addition, the forces that entered Chechnya in 1994 had been slapped together forming a rag-tag collection of various units. Lack of cohesion was an undisputed major Russian weakness. [64] Chaos, chance,

---

[63] Ibid, 24

[64] Ibid.

and friction dominate military operations as much today as when Clausewitz wrote about them after the Napoleonic wars. To reduce some of this chaos from the battlefield, commanders require the capability to execute mission command. Mission command is the exercise of authority and direction by the commander using mission orders to enable disciplined initiative within the commander's intent to empower leaders. Through mission command, commanders initiate all actions and integrate all military functions toward a common goal. The fundamental principles of mission command are: build cohesive teams through mutual trust, create shared understanding, provide a clear commander's intent, exercise disciplined initiative, use mission orders, and accept prudent risk. Commanders at all levels need education, rigorous training, and experience at mission command in order to succeed in hybrid warfare.

Conclusion

With this research, the monograph attempted to identify what are the fundamental core skills a brigade combat team should focus on during their train/ready cycle in order to defeat a hybrid threat given a 12-24 month training period. In order to answer this question the author provided a review of U.S. Army training doctrine and how it drives the development of the brigade combat team's training strategy, a review of current professional and academic thoughts on the hybrid threat, and the analysis of two hybrid conflicts to identify reoccurring competencies required to defeat a hybrid threat.

While the core principle of Army training doctrine is preparation for full spectrum operations, it still only provides for how to effectively execute training, not how to effectively decide on what to train. Training doctrine does not provide a link between specific training tasks found in the Combined Arms Training Strategies and the hybrid threat. No methodology exists to allow commanders to crosswalk the characteristics or competencies of a hybrid threat to a task found within training doctrine. Without the professional and academic discourse on hybrid threats and historical military examples integrated into doctrine, commanders cannot be expected to

30

think critical about what to train in order to prepare for an adversary like the hybrid threat. These two factors provide the commander with the understanding to frame the operational environment in order to allow them to narrow down the over 300 collective tasks that can be found in the Combined Arms Training Strategies. Without this understanding, commanders will not be able to build a manageable Full Spectrum Operations Mission Essential Task List. Constraints on time and resources force commanders to make difficult decisions about what tasks units train in preparation for full spectrum operations. Doctrine forces commanders to make decisions on what to train based on their professional experiences. What happens when a commander does not have the experience? The U.S. Army cannot assume every leader has all the experience required to make these types of decisions. This is why research like this monograph is required outside of doctrine. The research conducted for this monograph is providing commanders with a base of knowledge to assist in critically thinking about the correct training tasks to be trained in preparation for a hybrid threat.

U.S. Army training doctrine only provides a broad overview of the hybrid threat. To deeper understand the hybrid threat, a literary review was required. The literary review within this monograph provides the reader with some of the discourse required to help develop a deeper understanding of what the hybrid threat means to the brigade combat team. In sum, existing literature regarding hybrid threats illustrates that future threats will utilize all means available to achieve their ends. The rise of hybrid warfare presents a complicating factor for the brigade combat team's leadership. The brigade combat team will need to develop a training strategy that addresses state and non-state actors that employ a range of what could be considered conventional and irregular capabilities. The training will also need to defend against a threat who will exploit success with both modern military capabilities and less sophisticated capabilities like the improvised explosive device. Additionally, the brigade combat team will need to train against irregular and conventional formations. The hybrid threat will employ guerrilla type ambushes one day while engaging in fixed formations conducting conventional attacks the next. This will

31

require the brigade combat team to develop the situation through action. Technology cannot deliver everything that a brigade combat team must learn about the environment and enemy organizations. Brigade combat teams must be prepared to develop the situation through action. Units must have the ability to learn and adapt based on interactions with partners, the enemy, and civilian populations.

The review of the 2006 Lebanon War between Israel and Hezbollah and the 1994 Chechen War between Russia and Chechen rebels serves as the historical military examples in order to provide a linkage between the tasks found in the Combined Arms Training Strategies and the tasks required to train to defeat a hybrid threat. The problems faced by both Israel and Russia with confronting hybrid threats were reviewed in the above assessments. The research exposed several deficiencies that led to the poor performances by both Israel and Russian forces in their respective conflict. These deficiencies prevented Israeli and Russian forces from achieving success on the battlefield. The analysis of both conflicts suggests there are five skill sets that form the core capabilities required to defeat a hybrid threat. These deficiencies were habitually found in research documents on both the 2006 Lebanon and 1994 Chechen Wars. In addition, these core skills can be found in existing after action reviews and articles that have and continue to come out of Iraq and Afghanistan.[65] This shows how universal these tasks are to success on the battlefield against any type of threat. The core skill sets include;

- Combined Arms Maneuver

- Offensive Operation in an Urban Environment

- Intelligence, Surveillance, and Reconnaissance that can collect on a broad array of information

---

[65]Ed Peskie, Aaron Schwengler, and David Fivecoat, "Tactical Adjustments," *Infantry Magazine* (June-August 2011): 26-30.

- Precision fires

- Mission Command on the move

As described in the 2006 Lebanon War section above, Israel's failure against Hezbollah demonstrates the risk of neglecting combined arms maneuver for an extended period. Our current force is well trained for stability operations and counterinsurgency, but our junior Officers and Soldiers are untrained in combined arms maneuver tasks required to conduct offense and defensive operations. Major General Michael S. Tucker, Commanding General of the 2nd Infantry Division, made the same point in his article, *Maintaining the Combat Edge*.[66] When called upon to conduct major combat operations against a hybrid threat, the Israeli Defense Force failed to achieve tactical, operational, or strategic success. The failure to train on combined arms maneuver is the most documented and stated cause for the failure of the Israeli forces in 2006. Israel also acknowledged this training shortfall in their after action reviews. Israel initiated a new defense plan called Teffen 2012 following the failure of the 2006 Lebanon war. Part of the plan called for a new emphasis on going back to the basics and focusing on combined arms fire and maneuver tactics and skills.[67]

The U.S. Army is at a critical tipping point because the expertise and experience with these skill sets resides with senior noncommissioned officers and senior field grade officers. Additionally, maneuvering mounted forces to close with and destroy the enemy through direct and indirect fire is quickly becoming a lost art. The current brigade combat team is good at operating at the independent platoon level, but they cannot operate as a maneuver element in an integrated combined arms force. It has been years since platoons have maneuvered as part of a

---

[66] Major General Michael S. Tucker, "Maintaining the combat Edge," *Military Review* (May-June 2011): 10.

[67] RAND, *Preparing and Training for the Full Spectrum of Military Challenges*, (Santa Monica: RAND, 2008), 207.

larger company or battalion formation over extended distances and time.[68] The Army will lose the institutional knowledge of Desert Storm and Operation Iraqi Freedom I, if brigade combat teams do not effectively train and mentor their junior leaders on these skills while the Army still has the institutional knowledge within its ranks.

The urban environment provided the backdrop for both conflicts. Hybrid threats like those of Hezbollah or Chechen rebels, will exploit complex and urban terrain in order to mitigate the brigade combat team's capabilities. Urbanization is a growing trend that cannot be ignored. The two most mentioned future threats to the United States are China and Iran. Both of these two countries have large urban populations. Fifty one percent of China's population is urbanized as of 2011. Sixty six percent of Iran's population lives within an urban setting. Russian forces took heavy casualties in Grozny and through their tactics, virtually destroyed the city.[69] One reason for the high Russian casualties was that they were unprepared for urban operations. Russian forces trained for mountain combat, small-scale counterterrorist actions, and even for urban defense, but not for capturing a populated area by force. The Russians did seemingly prepare for the attack, including encircling and cutting off the city. But the plans failed to take into account the resistance that would be encountered.[70] Urban terrain causes a spatially compressed battlefield that is not easily controlled by graphic control measures. Situational awareness becomes more complex because the brigade combat team needs to have situational awareness above the ground, at ground level, as well as below the ground. The threat becomes less apparent in the urban environment. Beyond the physical complexities of urban terrain, the addition of noncombatants increases the difficulty of combat. Maps simply do not accurately represent the complexity of

---

[68] Major General Michael S. Tucker, "Maintaining the combat Edge," *Military Review* (May-June 2011): 12.

[69] MJ Orr, *The Russian Ground Forces & Reform 1992-2002*, (Conflict Studies Research Institute Centre, 2003), 1-8.

[70] Olga Oliker, *Russia's Chechen Wars 1994-2000*, (Santa Monica: RAND, 2001),84.

urban terrain. Applying combat power in urban terrain increases the possibility of negative effects. The ability of Hezbollah and the Chechens to blend into the civilian populace made target discrimination very difficult for Israeli and Russian soldiers. This also forced the soldiers to make ethical decisions when they pulled the trigger.

Timely, reliable, accurate, and relevant intelligence support to the commander remains a prerequisite for conducting successful operations. Russian intelligence staffs and their commanders failed to adequately define the operating environment and describe its effects, and evaluate the Chechen threat. Insufficient maps and imagery products, inadequate intelligence preparation of the battlefield processes, and poor reconnaissance shrouded the Chechen capabilities. As a result, Russian commanders viewed their operational plan through an intelligence lens distorted not only by the fog of war, but also by the blinding light of their own arrogance, misperceptions, and predilections.[71] Israel faced the same difficulties in Lebanon. Israeli units were expected to reach objectives without the proper intelligence about the nature of the threat these units would face. When these forces reached their objectives Hezbollah's superior preparation, sophisticated tactics, and advance firepower surprised them.[72] All operations whether offensive, defensive, or counterinsurgency begins with proper reconnaissance and intelligence gathering of the environment.

The ability to integrate fires into the maneuver plan is also critical skill set that must be trained. The Israel Defense forces tried to use standoff air and artillery attacks to counter the rocket attacks by Hezbollah. This did not stop the attacks on Israel or result in the return of the Israeli soldiers whose capture had precipitated the war. Eventually Israel was required to enter Lebanon. Israel was not prepared to integrate these assets into the maneuver units. Prior to the

---

[71] Brian A. Kelly, *Intelligence Support to Military Operations on Urban Terrain: Lessons Learned from the Battle of Grozny*, (Carlisle Barracks, PA: U.S. War College, 2000), 32.

[72] RAND, *Preparing and Training for the Full Spectrum of Military Challenges*, (Santa Monica: RAND, 2008), 219.

35

war most of the forces would engage in low intensity conflict and counter terrorism training. This lack of preparation was evident with the use of field artillery and air assets because they were used exclusively for attacks on preplanned targets and rarely on the support of ground forces. The older soldiers with experience in Israel's 1980s era intervention into Lebanon were often the only members of the Defense Forces who had experience and training in critical skills such as close air support, field artillery, or mortars.[73] There has been less demand for indirect fires. Fire support in counterinsurgency and stability operations being conducted in Iraq and Afghanistan requires a much smaller volume of fires than required for offensive and defensive operations. Our operational capability to conduct high intensity fighting operations other than counterinsurgency has atrophied over the last 10 years. Because of collateral damage considerations and target sets that do not require a large volume of fire, units seldom mass fires at the battery level or higher in stability or counterinsurgency operations.[74] Three former brigade commanders wrote a white paper titled "The King and I," to highlight the atrophied skills of the Army's artillery branch to perform its basic warfighting functions. The authors point out that the fighting in Iraq and Afghanistan has forced artillery units to carry out missions other than their core functions. As Israel's experience has shown in Lebanon, in order to close with and destroy the enemy maneuver units require the skill to integrate field artillery and air support on targets while conducting offensive operations.

A new approach to command and control is required when facing a hybrid threat like Hezbollah or Chechen rebels. Brigade combat teams need the ability to operate decentralized and distributed on the future battlefield. Leader and staff training needs to emphasize creating an

---

[73] Ibid., 218.

[74] Sean McFarland, Michael Shields, and Jeffery Snow, "The King and I: The impending crisis in the Field Artillery to provide Fire Support to the Maneuver Commander," White Paper, http://www.npr.org/documents/2008/may/artillerywhitepaper.pdf (accessed November 14, 2011).

understanding of mission command in order to develop operational adaptability.[75] Command post exercise for staffs are crucial to helping the commander with visualizing, describing, directing, and assessing operations. Command post exercises help staffs develop the skills required to command and control formations along the spectrum of conflict. U.S. Army command posts operating in Iraq and Afghanistan have become permanent locations. The ability to command on the move has atrophied because the current operating environment does not require the command post to jump or command on the move because of static positions. Commanders have come to expect near perfect situational awareness prior to making a decision. Such information is often only available within a static command post with fixed robust communications, computers, intelligence, surveillance, and reconnaissance architecture. The Israel Defense Force relied too heavily on technology. Israeli leaders allowed commanders to command from their plasma screens rather than personally experience the battlefield. This stemmed from the supposed quality of intelligence or information that their command posts could provide rather than willingness to circulate on the battlefield.[76] Brigade combat teams must ensure that their subordinate leaders can make decisions based on what the forward commander can observe, sense, and hear on the radio.

The good news is that the U.S. Army does recognize the above core skills as being critical to conducting full spectrum operations. The above skills are identified as required capabilities for the force in the *United States Army Operating Concept, 2016-2018*.[77] In addition, Army doctrine identifies the importance of these skills as evident by the release of *Army Doctrine Publication 3-0, Unified Land Operations* were combined arms maneuver is an Army core competency required to achieve a physical, temporal, or psychological advantage over the enemy

---

[75] General Martin E. Dempsey, "Mission Command", *The Cavalry & Armor Journal*, (November-December, 2011): 6.

[76] Kober, "The Israel Defense Forces in the Second Lebanon War," *Perspectives:The Begin-Sadat Center for Strategic Studies*. Perspective Paper no. 22 (28 September 2006). 19.

[77] U.S. Army, *The U.S. Army Capstone Concept* (Fort Monroe: Headquarters, Department of the Army, 2011). 9.

by applying elements of combat power in a complementary manner.[78] These skill sets can also be identified within the Training and Doctrine Command institutions as well. The establishment of the Mission Command Center of Excellence at Fort Leavenworth, Kansas shows the emphasis being placed on mission command. The Mission Command Center of Excellence was established to lead the execution of the Mission Command Warfighting Function. It is responsible for providing a balanced and comprehensive approach to developing capabilities that advance both the art and science mission command.[79] Though the U.S. Army recognizes that these core skills are required, it does not link these skills as a requirement to train them when preparing for a hybrid threat. The second shortfall in training doctrine is that these skills are not emphasized over any of the other several hundred training tasks required to be trained by a combat brigade team. The tension that exists for commanders developing training strategy is that of prioritization. As outlined in the training doctrine section of this monograph, Army doctrine does not prioritize training tasks and time is limited. The last section of this monograph will address the topic of developing performance proficiency and the importance of prioritization of these skill sets over other training priorities.

Recommendations

In the above research, the question of what is the core skill sets required to defeat a hybrid threat such as Hezbollah is answered. The core tasks of collecting timely, accurate, and relevant intelligence in order to conduct operations in an urban environment among non-combatants using combined arms maneuver and directing it through mission command is the capability the U.S. Army requires to defeat a hybrid threat like Israel and Russia did in their

---

[78] U.S. Army, *Army Doctrine Publication 3-0, Unified Land Operations, 2011* (Washington: Headquarters, Department of the Army, 2011), 6.

[79] Mission Command Center of Excellence, Home Page, http://usacac.army.mil/cac2/MCCOE/ (accessed 12 January 2012).

respective conflicts. The tension that now exists is that of time. Does the Army need to prioritize these critical tasks above the other important tasks required to execute full spectrum operations?

The Army's position is to prepare across the full spectrum of operations, without prioritizing between them. ADP 3-0, *Unified Land Operations* states that the central idea of Unified Land Operations is for the Army to seize, retain, and exploit the initiative to gain and maintain a position of relative advantage in sustained land operations through offensive, defensive, stability operations or defense support of civil authorities.[80] The Army's position is clear that there is no prioritization to missions. The Army needs to operate across the spectrum of conflict and among all operational themes. However, without a prioritization from the Army, how does the brigade combat team manage time for training when it comes to developing the ability to execute across the full spectrum of operations without creating a capabilities gap due to a lack of prioritization? This is critical since brigade combat teams do not have unlimited time. The train/ready cycle in addition to the leadership manning cycle is only 24 months before the cycle is interrupted. Personnel turnover experienced at the end of the cycle reduces the unit's Mission Essential Task List proficiency level due to the transitions of outgoing and incoming personnel.

In order to understand why brigade combat teams need to prioritize training tasks, it is important to examine the time it requires to become proficient on these tasks. One thing that clearly emerges when looking at research on developing outstanding performance in any skill set is that all superb performance requires intense practice. The amount and quality of practice are two key factors in developing expertise. There are no short cuts in developing proficiency at a skill. The journey is not for the impatient.

Brigade combat teams cannot reach a level of expertise during a single train/ready cycle according to research on performance training. Scientists who have studied expertise and top

---

[80] U.S. Army, *Army Doctrine Publication 3-0, Unified land Operations, 2011* (Washington: Headquarters, Department of the Army, 2011), 1.

performance in a wide variety of domains have concluded it could take at least a decade to achieve expertise in a particular skill set, therefore only a level of proficiency should be the goal.[81] Proficiency defined as having the necessary ability, knowledge, or skill to do something successfully. In developing proficiency in a particular task, there is no agreed upon amount of required time. In examining research on performance training, the spectrum of time required to gain proficiency ranges from approximate 750 training hours to 10 years.[82] The brigade combat team is not trying to develop "chess masters" but trying to reach a level of proficiency. Army training doctrine states that units reach proficiency through repeated practice of tasks to standard. In addition, units must continue to train these tasks in order to prevent peaks and valleys within the training "Band of Excellence."

If time was not a resource constraint, training for all contingencies would be a feasible course of action. However, the Army has acknowledged that we are in an era of persistent conflict and this era will continue until at least 2028.[83] This statement demonstrates that the Army does not see our operational tempo decreasing any time soon. In addition, the decade leading up to the Iraq and Afghanistan conflicts was not a time of unlimited training time for the Army. The 1990s were also a time of persistent conflict for our military forces. In 1991, the United States had 600,000 soldiers deployed in support of Operations Desert Shield/Storm. The Army was involved in Somalia as well as Haiti, Bosnia, subsequent deployments to Kuwait in 1994 and 1998, and the Kosovo campaign in 1999.[84] Therefore, it is reasonable to conclude that future operational tempo

---

[81] Ericisson Anders, Michael Prietula, and Edward Cokely, "The Making of an Expert," *Harvard Business Review* (2006): 2.

[82] U.S. Army doctrine defines "Trained" as the unit demonstrating a proficiency in accomplishing the task to the Army standard.

[83] U.S. Army, *The U.S. Army Capstone Concept*, (Fort Monroe: Headquarters, Department of the Army, 2009), 12.

[84] Thomas Donnelly and Fredrick Kagan, *Ground Truth: The Future of U.S. Land Power*. (Washington, D.C.: AEI Press, 2008), 8.

will continue to limit available training time; therefore, units must prioritize training to ensure the core skills required for a hybrid threat is trained before any other training is considered.

The minimum scientific documented amount of time required to reach a level of proficiency that this research has found is 750hrs. If units use 750 hours as the baseline for the amount of training hours it requires to reach a level of proficiency in a specific collective task, brigade combat teams could only train 1-2 collective tasks per quarterly training cycle.[85] This would equal a maximum of 4-8 skill sets that could be developed in an annual training cycle. This is only accounting for the collective training required to develop the recommend hybrid threat core skill sets. Brigade combat teams would still need to allocate time for individual and leader training that would need to be trained in order to begin building the foundation before moving on to collective training. In addition, this does not factor in any other training required by *Army Regulations 350-1, Training in Units*. A brigade combat team's time is very limited when you begin to add up the requirements of individual, leader, collective training, maintenance requirements, and other administrative requirements. The challenge of preparedness is not new. The relevant question for the brigade combat team remains how to prioritize action. The identification of time requirements is vital to developing this training strategy. Identifying the required time it takes to develop training proficiency is important because it provides the unit with a baseline to begin allocating time within the training calendar in order to protect this training time.

Over the last decade, the operational side of the Army had to learn to fight the counterinsurgency fight in Iraq and Afghanistan. Moreover, as the Army became embroiled in these wars, less emphasis was paid to the conventional war and its emphasis of combined arms maneuver. There is an intellectual tension about which way the Army should train and equip for the next war (and there will always be a next war). It has long been the opinion of many military

---

[85] This is based on a 12 hour training day given 20 training days per month.

intellects that the Army needs to maintain that heavy, conventional war of maneuver capability. This view insists that it is a lot easier for a heavy maneuver unit to downshift to counterinsurgency operations than for a light counterinsurgency force to fight on a heavy maneuver battlefield.[86]

Further, look at the pace of operations in Desert Storm versus the current war in Iraq or Afghanistan. The fact is the Army has to get it right the first time in a war with a near-peer enemy. The Army will not get a second chance. However, in a counterinsurgency fight, the brigade combat team has time to make mistakes, readjust the force, and reshape the battlefield. Let us take Iran for an example. If U.S. Army would end up having to fight them, will it be a conventional war, or a counterinsurgency war? Iran has a large conventional army. It also has a large pseudo-army, the Iranian Revolutionary Guard Corps. What might a war with Iran look like? It would look a lot like the invasion of Iraq in 2003. It would begin with a rather conventional fight, and only after U.S. forces won the conventional fight would it turn to a guerrilla campaign.

The review of the 2006 Lebanon War and the 1994/1996 Chechnya War suggests that there are five skill sets vital to success in defeating a hybrid threat like Hezbollah or the Chechen rebels. The research on performance proficiency shows that training priorities are required because of the time it takes to reach a level of proficiency in a particular skill. Therefore, brigade combat teams should prioritize the identified skill sets of combined arms maneuver, offensive operation in an urban environment, intelligence, surveillance, and reconnaissance that can collect on a broad array of information, precision fires, and mission command on the move over all other training until a level of proficiency has been met. As the 2006 Lebanon War has shown, when states focus their armies on doing nothing but counterinsurgency and world constabulary missions

---

[86] Guy Ruz, "Army Forces Focus on Counterinsurgency Debate Within" http://www.npr.org/templates/story/story.php?storyId=90200038 (accessed October 24, 2011).

to the exclusion of preparing for conventional warfare, strategic and operational failure can result. Granted, stability missions will be revisited by our armed forces and the Army must be prepared to execute them, but in a world of limited resources and time, hard choices must be made in terms of how a brigade combat team trains. The choice should be to build a brigade combat team on the principle of fighting. From there it should follow that the ability to step in other directions and to perform missions such as counterinsurgency and/or stability operations comes from the ability to fight. [87]

---

[87] Gian P. Gentile, "Let's Build an Army to Win All Wars", *Joint Forces Quarterly*, 52 (1st Quarter 2009): 27.

Bibliography

Aldis, Anne. *The Second Chechen War.* United Kingdom: Strategic & Combat Studies Institute, 2000.

Archar, Gilbert and Michel Warschawski. *The 33-Day War: Israel's War on Hezbollah in Lebanon and its Consquences.* Boulder: Paradigm Publishing, 2007.

Bacon, Lance M. *Army Annouces Switch to 9 Month deployments.* August 5, 2011. http://www.armytimes.com/news/2011/08/army-nine-month-deployments-080511w/ (accessed September 13, 2011).

Bank, Stephen J., and Jr. Earl H. Tilford. *Russia's Invasion of Chechnya: A Preliminary Assessment.* Special Report, Carisle: Strategic Studies Institute, 1995.

Cone, General Rober W. "Shaping the Army of 2020." *Army Magazine*, 2011: 71-76.

Farquhar, Lieutenant Colonel Scott C. *Back to Basics: A Study of the Second Lebanon War and Operation CAST LEAD.* Leavenworth: Combat Studies Institute Press, 2009.

Friedman, Stephen Biddle, and Jeffrey A. Friedman. *The 2006 Lebanon Campaign and the Future of Warfare: Implications for Army and Defense Policy.* Carlisle: Strategic Studies Institute, 2008.

Gentile, Gian P. "Let's Build an Army to Win All Wars." *Joint Forces Quarterly, 1st Quarter 2009*: 27-33.

Glenn, Russell W. *All Glory is Fleeting: Insights from the Second Lebanon War.* Santa Monica: RAND, 2008.

Hoffman, Frank G. *Conflict in the 21st Century: The Rise of Hybrid Wars.* Arlington: Potomac Institiute for Policy Studies, 2007.

Hoffman, Frank G. "Hybrid Threats: Reconceptualizing the Evolving Character of Modern Conflict." *Strategic Forum*, 2009: 1-9.

HQs, Department of the Army, U.S. *Field Manual, 3-0, Operations.* Washington, D.C.: Department of the Army, 2011.

HQs, Department of the Army, U.S. *Field Manual, 7-0, Training Units and Developing Leaders for Full Spectrum Operatioins.* Washington, D.C.: Department of the Army, 2011.

HQs, Department of the Army, U.S. *Training Circular, 7-100, Hybrid Threat.* Washington, D.C.: Department of the Army, 2010.

Hybrid Warfare. Briefing to the Subcommittee on Terrorism, Unconventional Threats and Capabilities, Committee on Armed Services, House of Representatives. Washington D.C.: Government Accounting Office, 2010.

Jenkinson, Brett C. MAJ. "Tactical Observations from the Grozny Combat Experience." Masters Thesis, U.S. Army Command and General Staff College, 2002.

Joes, Anthony James. *Urban Guerrilla Warfare.* Lexington: The University Press of Kentucky, 2007.

Johnson, Daveid E. *Military Capabilities for Hybrid War Insights from the Israel Defense Forces in Lebanon and Gaza,* Santa Monica: RAND, 2010.

Johnson, MAJ Mark E. "The Chechen Conflict: A Case for U.S. Intervention." Masters Monograph, U.S. Army Command and General Staff College, School of Advance Military Studies, 2006.

Kagan, Thomas Donnelly and Fredrick. *Ground Truth: The Future of U.S. Land Power.* Washington, D.C.: AEI Press, 2008.

Keller, Brian A. *Intelligence Support to Military Operations on Urban Terrain: Lessons Learned from the Battle of Grozny.* Research Project, Carlisle Barracks: U.S. Army War College, 2000.

Keller, LTC Brian. *Intelligence Support to Military Operations on Urban Terrain: Lessons Learned from the Battle of Gronzy.* Strategic Research Project, Carisle: U.S. Army War College, 2000.

Kenney, J. Q. *"Are We Prepared for Hybrid Warfare?"* Issue Paper, Quantico: United States Marine Corps,Command and Staff College, 2008.

Knezys, Stasys, and Romanas Sedlickas. *The War in Chechnya.* College Station: Texas A&M Universtiy Press, 2000.

Kober, Avi. "The Israel Defense Forces in the Second Lebanon War: Why the Poor Performance?" *Journal of Strategic Studies*, 2008: 3-40.

Lasica, Lt Col Daniel T. *Strategic Implications of Hybrid War: A Theory of Victory.* Masters Monograph, U.S. Army Command and General Staff College, School of Advance Military Studies, 2009.

Lieven, Anatol. *Chechnya: Tombstone of Russian Power.* New Haven: Yale Univesity Press, 1998.

Matthews, Matt. *We Were Caught Unprepared: The 2006 Hezbollah-Israeli War.* Fort Leavenworth: U.S. Army Combined Arms Center Combat Studies Institute Press, 2008.

McWilliams, MAJ Sean J. "Hybrid War Beyond Lebanon: Lessons from the South African Campaign 1976 to 1989." Masters Monograph, U.S. Army Command and General Staff College, School of Advance Military Studies, 2009.

Meier, Andrew. *Chechnya: To the Heart of a Conflict.* New York: W.W. Norton & Company, 2005.

Mercur, James. *Elements of the Art of War: Prepared for the Use of the Cadets of the United States Military Academy.* New York: John Wiley & Sons, 1894.

Murphy, Brian J. "No Heroic Battles: Lessons of the Second Lebanon War." Masters Thesis, U.S. Army Command and General Staff College, 2010.

Oliker, Olga. *Russia's Chechen Wars 1994-2000.* Santa Monica: Rand, 2001.

Politkovskaya, Ann. *A Small Corner of Hell: Dispatches from Chechnya.* Chicago: The Universtiy of Chicago Press, 2004.

RAND. *Preparing and Training for the Full Specturm of Military Challenges.* Santa Monica: RAND, 2009.

Russel, John. *Chechnay - Russia's "War on Terror."* New York: Routledge, 2007.

Simpson, Erin M. "Thinking about Modern Conflict: Hybrid Wars, Strategy, and War Aims." Paper presented at the annual meeting of the Midwest Political Science Association,Chicago, 2005.

Steele, Captain Matthew F. "The Conduct of War." *Journal of the Military Service Institution of the United States*, 1908: 22-31.

Stone, David R. *A Military History of Russia: From Ivan the Terrible to the War in Chechnya.* Westport: Praeger Security International, 2006.

Tucker, Michael S. "Maintaining the Combat Edge." *Military Review*, 2011: 8-15.

U.S., Department of Defense. *National Defense Strategy.* Washington, D.C.: Department of Defense, 2005.

Wagner, Arthur L. "Strategy" A Lecture Delivered by Colonel Arthur L. Waganer, Assistant Adjutant-General, U.S.A, to the Officers of the Regular Army and National Guard at the Maneuvers at West Point, KY., and at Fort Riley, Kansas, 1903. Kansas City: Hudson-Kimberly Publishing, 1903.